#happy

a quote book

by gloria marie pelcher

#happy: a quote book

ISBN-13: 978-0692331309 (Creative Bluebird)

ISBN-10: 0692331301

#quotebooks is a trademark of

Creative Bluebird
www.creativebluebird.com

For book inquiries please visit
creativebluebird.com/contact

for

_____

from

_____

date

_____

#happy

Here's to being happy! Life is filled with challenges, but as the saying goes…there are so many beautiful things to be happy about!

This life is yours. Take the power to choose what you want to do and do it well. Take the power to love what you want in life and love it honestly. Take the power to walk in the forest and be a part of nature. Take the power to control your own life. No one else can do it for you. Take the power to make your life happy.

Susan Polis Schutz

For every minute you are angry you lose sixty seconds of happiness.

Ralph Waldo Emerson

Folks are usually about as happy as they make their minds up to be.

Abraham Lincoln

When one door of happiness closes, another opens; but often we look so long at the closed door that we do not see the one which has been opened for us.

Helen Keller

I believe in pink. I believe that laughing is the best calorie burner. I believe in kissing, kissing a lot. I believe in being strong when everything seems to be going wrong. I believe that happy girls are the prettiest girls. I believe that tomorrow is another day and I believe in miracles.

Audrey Hepburn

Happiness is when what you think, what you say, and what you do are in harmony.

Mahatma Gandhi

Happiness is not something readymade. It comes from your own actions.

Dalai Lama XIV

I would always rather be
happy than dignified.

Charlotte Brontë

When I was 5 years old, my mother always told me that happiness was the key to life. When I went to school, they asked me what I wanted to be when I grew up. I wrote down 'happy'. They told me I didn't understand the assignment, and I told them they didn't understand life.

John Lennon

Think of all the beauty still
left around you and be happy.

Anne Frank

It isn't what you have or who you are or where you are or what you are doing that makes you happy or unhappy. It is what you think about it.

Dale Carnegie

Happiness is the consequence of personal effort. You fight for it, strive for it, insist upon it, and sometimes even travel around the world looking for it.

Elizabeth Gilbert

Success is getting what you want, happiness is wanting what you get.

W.P. Kinsella

Learn to value yourself,
which means: fight for your
happiness.

Ayn Rand

It's been my experience that you can nearly always enjoy things if you make up your mind firmly that you will.

L.M. Montgomery

The grand essentials to happiness in this life are something to do, something to love, and something to hope for.

George Washington Burnap

But who can say what's best? That's why you need to grab whatever chance you have of happiness where you find it, and not worry about other people too much. My experience tells me that we get no more than two or three such chances in a life time, and if we let them go, we regret it for the rest of our lives.

Haruki Murakami

Happiness always looks small while you hold it in your hands, but let it go, and you learn at once how big and precious it is.

Maxim Gorky

The best way to cheer yourself is to try to cheer someone else up.

Mark Twain

Let no one ever come to you
without leaving better and
happier. Be the living
expression of God's kindness:
kindness in your face,
kindness in your eyes,
kindness in your smile.

Mother Teresa

So we shall let the reader answer this question for himself: who is the happier man, he who has braved the storm of life and lived or he who has stayed securely on shore and merely existed?

Hunter S. Thompson

One of the keys to happiness is a bad memory.

Rita Mae Brown

If you want to be happy, be.

Leo Tolstoy

Cry. Forgive. Learn. Move on. Let your tears water the seeds of your future happiness.

Steve Maraboli

#

Now and then it's good to
pause in our pursuit of
happiness and just be happy.

Guillaume Apollinaire

Happiness depends upon ourselves.

Aristotle

The real things haven't changed. It is still best to be honest and truthful; to make the most of what we have; to be happy with simple pleasures; and have courage when things go wrong.

Laura Ingalls Wilder

I must learn to be content
with being happier than I
deserve.

Jane Austen

We don't make mistakes, just happy little accidents.

Bob Ross

From the backstabbing co-worker to the
meddling sister-in-law, you are in charge of
how you react to the people and events in your
life. You can either give negativity power over
your life or you can choose happiness instead.
Take control and choose to focus on what is
important in your life. Those who cannot live
fully often become destroyers of life.

Anaïs Nin

Generally speaking, the most miserable people I know are those who are obsessed with themselves; the happiest people I know are those who lose themselves in the service of others...By and large, I have come to see that if we complain about life, it is because we are thinking only of ourselves.

Gordon B. Hinckley

Happiness is like a butterfly which, when pursued, is always beyond our grasp, but, if you will sit down quietly, may alight upon you.

Nathaniel Hawthorne

The happiness of your life
depends upon the quality of
your thoughts.

Marcus Aurelius

The secret of happiness is freedom, the secret of freedom is courage.

Carrie Jones

I think happiness is what
makes you pretty. Period.
Happy people are beautiful.
They become like a mirror
and they reflect that
happiness.

Drew Barrymore

A mathematical formula for happiness: Reality divided by Expectations. There were two ways to be happy: improve your reality or lower your expectations.

Jodi Picoult

Sometimes, we just have to be happy with what people can offer us. Even if it's not what we want, at least it's something.

Sarah Dessen

People want pretty much the same things: They wanted to be happy. Most young people seemed to think that those things lay somewhere in the future, while most older people believed they lay in the past.

Nicholas Sparks

So come with me, where dreams are born, and time is never planned. Just think of happy things, and your heart will fly on wings, forever, in Never Never Land!

J.M. Barrie

Yesterday is dead, tomorrow hasn't arrived yet. I have just one day, and I'm going to be happy in it.

Groucho Marx

The greater part of our happiness or misery depends upon our dispositions, and not upon our circumstances.

Martha Washington

True happiness is to enjoy the present, without anxious dependence upon the future, not to amuse ourselves with either hopes or fears but to rest satisfied with what we have, which is sufficient, for he that is so wants nothing. The greatest blessings of mankind are within us and within our reach. A wise man is content with his lot, whatever it may be, without wishing for what he has not.

Seneca

Children are happy because they don't have a file in their minds called "All the Things That Could Go Wrong.

Marianne Williamson

If you want to live a happy life, tie it to a goal, not to people or things.

Albert Einstein

Happiness, not in another
place but this place...not for
another hour, but this hour.

Walt Whitman

The power of finding beauty
in the humblest things makes
home happy and life lovely.

Louisa May Alcott

Everyone wants to live on top of the mountain, but all the happiness and growth occurs while you're climbing it.

Andy Rooney

Action may not always bring happiness, but there is no happiness without action.

William James

Happiness can be found,
even in the darkest of times,
if one only remembers to
turn on the light.

Steve Kloves

Happiness is a risk. If you're not a little scared, then you're not doing it right.

Sarah Addison Allen

my favorite happy quote

_____
_____
_____
_____
_____
_____
_____
_____
_____
_____

A B O U T this book

THIS BOOK that you are holding in your hands was made with love by GLORIA MARIE PELCHER. This book is part of the *#quotebooks*™ collection of books. This book is perfectly okay with being loved, bought, read, reread, shared, gifted, tweeted, instagrammed, liked, reviewed, borrowed, and of course quoted.

gloriamarie.com/quotebooks

FB / IG / Twitter: @gloriamarie

Printed in Great Britain
by Amazon.co.uk, Ltd.,
Marston Gate.